THE CRACKER BOX POEMS

THE CRACKER BOX POEMS

Joe Benevento

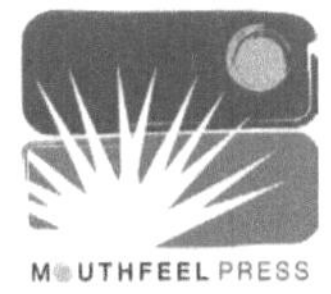

MOUTHFEEL PRESS

Huntsville | El Paso, Texas

Mouthfeel Press is an indie press publishing works in English and Spanish by new and established poets. We publish poetry, fiction, and non-fiction. Our books are available through our website, Amazon.com, Bookshop.org, and other online and independent bookseller,
or at author's readings.

Cover Design: Karen Dreher

Contact information:
Mouthfeelbooks.com
Info.mouthfeelbooks@gmail.com

ISBN: 978-1-957840-03-1
Library of Congress Control Number: 2022945809

Published in the United States, 2023

First Printing in English

ACKNOWLEDGEMENTS

"After the Boys Goaded Me and Ricky Irizarry into a Fistfight," *The Wax Paper*

"Catholic School Stories You Maybe Haven't Heard," "Three Inch Heels," *Rabid Oak*

"After Richie Simonson's Mother Threw Away Our Rock Collection," "Bobwhite on Our Back Lawn," "After We Noticed the Little Red Bud Tree," *Poetry Pacific*

"After Uncle Louie Got Me on Some Nights at the Daily News," *Waterwheel*

"After My Fiancée Was Too Busy to Attend the Italian Club's Spring Festa," *Botticelli Magazine*

"I Make My Father Some Hard-Boiled Eggs," *Evening Street Review*

"Fohey and Joey," *Daybreak*

"Apricots," *The Griffin*

"After I Left the Hospital Having Witnessed the Birth of My First Child," "The Plant in My Office," *Last Stanza*

"Sudden Rain," *Heart*

"After Seeing My Son Dance a Tarantella in Fairfield, Iowa," "After Taking the Wrong I-480 Out of Omaha," *Oakwood*

"Pasta Three Times a Week," *Blue Collar Review*

"After Margaret Did Not Believe How Soon Forsythias Turn Green," *Verdad*

"The Silence of the Wrens," *Calliope*

"I Hit a Squirrel with a Child's Green Plastic Watering Can," *Schuykill Valley Journal*

"Afib and the Fly," *Tipton Poetry Journal*

"Mrs. Barber's Memory," *Words and Whispers*

"After Singing 'Volare' With an Actual Italian," "Ode to January," *I-70 Review*

CONTENTS

WORK AND CLASS — 9
After Marilyn Meshak Zipped Up My Pants — 11
After the Boys Goaded Me and Ricky Irizarry into a Fistfight — 12
Catholic School Stories You Maybe Haven't Heard — 13
After Richie Simonson's Mother Threw Away Our Rock Collection — 15
After Uncle Louie Got Me on Some Nights at the Daily News — 16
Three Inch Heels — 17
The Problem with Moths — 19
The Dobermans — 20
After My Fiancée Was Too Busy to Attend the Italian Club's Spring Festa — 21
After the Last Blue-Collar Job — 22
I Make My Father Some Hard-Boiled Eggs — 23
Five Days Before His 91st Birthday — 24
After My Brother Claimed I Was Tough — 25
After My First Bad Slice of Pizza — 26

TEACHER AND CHILDREN — 27
Song — 29
Fohey and Joey — 30
Apricots — 31
After I Left the Hospital Having Witnessed the Birth of My First Child — 32
Sudden Rain — 33
The Plant in My Office — 34
After Seeing My Son Dance a Tarantella in Fairfield, Iowa — 35
After We Noticed the Little Redbud Tree — 36
Bobwhite on Our Back Lawn — 37
Solo — 38
Pasta Three Times a Week — 39
$40 Cake — 40
I Wear an Eight Dollar Watch — 41
Mrs. Barber's Memory — 42
After Having That Italian Pastry Dream for About the Hundredth Time — 43
After Keith and I Stopped Meeting in front of Macy's on Christmas Eve — 44
After Margaret Did Not Believe How Soon Forsythias Turn Green — 45

THE CRACKER BOX   47

After We Finally Called the Bat Men   49

After Taking the Wrong I-480 Out of Omaha   50

The Pit Bulls of East Oakland   51

The Silence of the Wrens   53

I Hit a Squirrel with a Child's Green Plastic Watering Can   54

After Claire Asked Me to Teach Her How to Play Guitar   55

A-Fib and the Fly   56

After Singing "Volare" with an Actual Italian   57

After Black Friday Began on a Thursday   58

Ode To January   59

If I Could Tell This Story   60

James's Dream   61

My Son Caught a Twelve Pound Grass Carp   62

I Want Out of the Cracker Box Too   63

AUTHOR'S BIOGRAPHY   67

WORK AND CLASS

After Marilyn Meshak Zipped Up My Pants

Because Marina Ramírez, one of our first grade classmates
at St. Teresa of Avila noticed my fly was undone, and Marilyn,
seeing me paralyzed with what would become chronic
embarrassment, could not wait for me to save myself,
her sympathy securing me against the others' jeers.

She never would suppose the crush I had already
decided even before she fingered the fly of my gold-
striped, chocolate brown pants, or the years
ahead of touching her, almost as when I umpired
close behind as she pitched seventh grade softball

or a year later when I came nearest to defeating
eight years of ineptitude by asking her to dance
to the deafening decibels of a heavy rock band,
where we frugged and fretted without
once managing to undo the space between us.

And each time her light blue eyes
might have been calling me to become
who I could not manage myself to be,
a peer, a protector, since I lacked
the knowledge that even Marilyns can have anguish,

might be waiting to have someone
secure them, not so much by promising
a perfect love, which can then never be,
as by being ready to step in if needed,
perhaps even offering a hand

all those times we have something we ought to keep hidden.

After the Boys Goaded Me and
Ricky Irizarry into a Fistfight

it all starting when Ricky hit my hatted head with a lit match,
one of many he was flinging just for fun as we exited
the Parish Hall after Thursday night basketball practice
for St. Teresa's eight grade team. He meant no harm, but everyone's
reaction, all the "Wow, man, you gonna take that?" questions they delivered

pressured me at least to comment, "You gotta be more careful, man,"
which I punctuated with the slightest push on his chest. Silly Ricky
waited until I turned away before pushing back, just as gently, so
I had to push our problem further by facing
him as I again made contact.

After the third time he waited to push me in the back,
the boys' phony indignation reaching each time further
for crescendo, Ricky made it impossible for us not to fight.
All our teammates, black, white, and Puerto Rican, united
as they rarely were, in love with the way this game was unfolding

with more drama than any overtime, framed us into hitting
each other's faces, our winter gloves the only cover for
our bare fists, our lack of skill or style no stop to the joy
our pals procured, seeing their two back up centers contend
way harder than we ever managed on the court. I fought furious,

my rage making me immune to the hard shots I received,
caught up in all the things I hated none of them named
Ricky Irizarry, so when they took us under the Parish Hall lights,
to judge who had delivered the better beating, I was declared
the winner, though, always a little smarter than poor Ricky,

I understood by how much I had lost.

Catholic School Stories You Maybe Haven't Heard

Every Catholic baby boomer shares the usual tales
about nuns or brothers and their punishments
too extreme to be ranked corporal.
Like Sister Rita Cathleen, who used to pull
out students' hair and then let us see
it descending from her fingers
to the classroom floor: her way to show us
she had gotten some.
Or Sister Jeremy, who once locked
little Billy Abruzzino in the dark
coat closet and left him there
for hours after school until his mother
found success in her desperate search.

But the harm I remember most
involved words. Like when Sister Clarisse
told us only the Irish "are God's people."
The rest of us Italians, Puerto Ricans, Polish,
and blacks were all a bunch of sinful losers.
Once, Sister Jeremy threatening
my Lithuanian friend Algis Oslapas during
Mass, promising, "If you don't shut up
Mr. Oslapas, I'm going to really make
you sloppy." Years later, Mr. Mitchell who
coached track, taught religion and classics
at Cathedral Prep, getting angry at me for quitting the team
and for the next four years insulting me at every
turn, sometimes in Latin, as when he borrowed
Cicero's speech against his hated enemy, substituting
my name for Cataline's, or when Mitchell told my classmate
Jamie Guevara, "Hey Guevara, you know the only
guy greasier in this school than you is Benevento."
I stuck to the Stoicism I had learned in his class,
never gave him an excuse to get me expelled (unlike
my hero Filipino friend Martin Del Rosario, who responded

to Mitchell's labeling of him as a "half-ass" with "Well, you're
a whole one"). Mitchell relented a little by senior year, even
warned me about my scholarship to NYU: "Watch out
for all those Jews."

You can recover from a hard slap in the face
and when you're a kid your hair grows back fast,
but what child can recover completely from the person
in charge of your education, who negates your name,
your complexion, your people, allowing you no way
to duck the blow, turn on the light, unlock
the door that might lead to your escape.

After Richie Simonson's Mother Threw Away Our Rock Collection

which included some pretty pink quartz, black and white granite,
and our favorite, a dull grey stone with a solid blue center,
(we both had sat on his unfinished basement's floor amazed
our hammering had unearthed that kept-in color)
we were upset that solid sign of our friendship

was gone, since the other boys
had derided us for wasting some summer
afternoons collecting dull, dirty rocks
from around our neighborhood to have
at them with hammers, cracking dull codes
to see what secrets were kept inside.

No safety goggles, no sense then
of danger; we just banged at them
until they broke, usually in a few pieces,
though a stray specimen of sandstone
might crumble to bits before our always

observant eyes. After a while we knew
what to expect, like fishing his uncle's
pond upstate for sunfish and bass—you
probably weren't going to pull out a rainbow
trout, still it didn't take more than one

blue center to keep us aware almost anything
could happen. This very next rock might shine
flecks of gold or hopeful bits of green beryl precious
to us, cementing our friendship on the dusty cellar
floor, until time, like someone's tidy mother,

would discard the evidence forever.

After Uncle Louie Got Me on Some
Nights at the Daily News

No cub reporter, instead one cog of a three-man crew
walking serpentine around the grimy floor to the drop
off spot for the giant rolls of unprocessed paper. One
precise push would conveyor belt them on their eventual
way to print. It was union work, but Louie Catapano,

veteran foreman, could call me up whenever they needed
an extra grunt, $10 per hour back when I was making $3
at my daytime factory job, so I could never say no thanks,
would just walk twelve blocks back to the A train, taking me
to eight to ten hours of easier money: forty-five minutes off

for every hour and a half we worked, unplanned stops whenever
the machinery wanted to rest, a mini-deli break room
open even at 3 AM, where I'd coffee or snack, though
some of the full-time crew preferred the bar just two
blocks down. One night into almost dawn I wrote

on a pocket-sized yellow pad with a blue Bic pen,
maybe ten love poems for Dorothy Lin, my latest
NYU crush, symbols I'd later copy on cleaner paper
to hand her my suffering, which she later handed back
in the most awkward telephone conversation of our lives, saying

"That was not what I meant at all." But I could not know
that yet, as I hoped between hard pushes or as I came close
to death, flying home with some co-worker from my part of Queens
who had spent his breaks at the bar, or even as I kept
blowing black soot out of my nose well into Saturday afternoon,

evidence too obvious, I figured, for an actual bad omen.

Three Inch Heels

for guys were in
among the Puerto Ricans
with whom I hung.
I didn't often digress
away from white
boy apparel, but somehow
succumbed, bought a pair,
which I didn't try to wear yet
walking with them hidden in their box
down Liberty Avenue towards home.

Got on with them on the Q41 for high
School, already 6'2 stockinged,
it was harder to step up
without hitting my head. The almost all white
boys and faculty at Cathedral Prep all wondering
what else was up beyond my stature. Father Keane
reminding me I was already tall, guys in the locker
room taking turns rising up, seeing what it was like
to walk a moment in my shoes.

Wore them one Saturday, 9-9 shift
at May Department Store, found out
what women suffered for fashion's sake
in those back-
breakers.

Finally, they fit in attending my best friend Jose's
high school graduation party. His parents going
all the way with a roast pig on a spit,
not a common sight in Queens, and pulpo
also on the menu—my first time seeing, much
less eating octopus.

Of course, there was dancing, and even though
my salsa steps were silly in those three-inch
heels, I at least looked the part un poco mejor.

And when I grinded with Irene Vargas
almost six feet before shoes herself,
black hair down to her cintura, each of us
higher than normal, hanging on each
other for balance, her perfume,
her summertime no air-conditioned sweat
pressed against me so close, I wanted to
stay in that space forever, though I knew
I'd never really be able to hold on, no matter
the inches closer I feigned being on top of things.

The Problem with Moths

The moth thinks he wants to get inside.
The light is here and late October nights
turn cold faster than he can fly.

He keeps his wings whirring
up and down the unforgiving glass,
which has no space to let him through.

He doesn't suspect if someone opened
the glass door and he entered that space
of brightness and warmth

he soon might be splattered, wings
wasted into sparkles against a wall
or even a grasping hand.

The safest place for a moth
is away from the light, the fire is never
his friend, even artificial light

an accomplice to court death
from a waiting list of predators:
bats, nighthawks, low-lying frogs.

Still the moth cannot resist.
Still the moth must be drawn to danger.
Still the moth cannot forestall his

inveterate, invertebrate fate.
Thoreau tells us "a person is rich in proportion
to the number of things he can afford to let alone."

So too the moth.

The Dobermans

I
My friend David worries about
the big black dog his new
neighbor doesn't restrain.
His daughter jogs. He and his wife
bike, fearing that dark attack
from behind, those powerful jaws,
tearing teeth, remorseless
as nightmares always are.

II
My older brother Frank has always
favored big dogs: a white German
shepherd who liked to kill cats,
a brindled grey Great Dane who once
took to tearing the siding off our house.
A sleek, black dog, not an ounce of forgiving
fat, until that dog took ill, had to be put
down. My tough guy brother shooting his
pet, crying for days after.

III
My former flame Hallene had
a Doberman and an erring husband.
One night at a party in their apartment
she closed the dog in a room
adjacent to the bathroom whose door
was also closed. Twice, more beer-logged
each time, I worried I'd open the wrong
door, but lived to laugh later about her
husband getting bit just after he had
demanded a divorce, as if that canine
knew it was finally all right to let
someone have it.

After My Fiancée Was Too Busy to Attend the Italian Club's Spring Festa

I was close to content, close to deciding Carmen
could not keep choosing her homework over me
without consequences. I was set to sing "La Mattinata"
a famous Italian love song my professor, Joe Italiano
(yes, really) had commissioned me to learn. His vision:

I'd enter the crowded room, guitar in hands, flanked by two co-
singing, co-eds in airy dresses to start the party.
I had no illusions about either blonde; instead, I would be
scanning the room for Christine Frangiapane, my classmate
for all three Italian classes we'd taken at NYU, a paisana

with a beau she also would not be bringing in from Brooklyn,
hers a Mafia wannabe stewing in Bensonhurst
about her bookishness, mine all too wrapped up in her
Biology major in Bay Ridge. Maybe it was time for Christine
and I to let our lips speak the words our mutually dark eyes

had imagined more than once when we teamed up for
flirty dialogue assignments we co-authored and performed,
maybe, Carmen-less, I would dance instead with Christine,
who I noticed, in an orange-red, disco-y dress she might have
maneuvered to tempt Travolta, just five seconds before I saw

my fiancée, who had six-sensed trouble, showing
up in time to assure Christine Frangiapane
would never teach me what she knew, my intended securing me
in an embrace lasting all through that April evening's
sure seduction away from Romantic might-have-beens,

towards a marriage that was destined to fail.

After the Last Blue-Collar Job

I still have nightmares, over thirty years later,
of Hammel-Riglander, a wholesale supply
house on Hudson Street where I worked
each summer after NYU: order-picker, stock-boy,
assistant order-checker, shipping department packer,

though they broke me back there, with all their ridicule
of how I mishandled merchandise boxing, so bad
I ran to the office, not holding back tears, told management
I quit, though Mr. Duel, with a slight college boy
of his own on the crew, talked me into remaining, knowing

how much I needed the money. Getting through those summer
and part-time jobs: sporting goods clerk at May Department Store,
plumber's helper in Harlem for my brother-in-law, part-time painter
of apartments he also owned, was a microcosm of my whole life
struggling to hide my misfit in the working class.

Times I was assigned to assemble a bicycle,
disembowel a toilet, set a sink, paint a wall
with steady, even strokes, or simply figure out
what best fit in a box, all failures confirming
my Brooklyn-born, hard worker father's nickname for me

"Da Genius," the kid who "couldn't tell a socket wrench
from a pair of pliers," who feared every new opportunity
to prove how little he knew about paint thinner, soldering
guns, box cutters, chip hammers, how little he longed to figure
out anything but how to earn enough money for the books,

the classes which might rescue him from too hard labor forever.

I Make My Father Some Hard-Boiled Eggs

I'm home just a week, all I can spare
from my life and children 1200 miles away,
back to help my mother learn how to use
her walker again, after weeks on her back
in the hospital.

But my dad needs me almost
as much; his sugar daily testing too high,
making him feel even weaker than his
almost ninety years.
My first morning back, I see him consume
a jumbo corn muffin, bagel, butter, orange
juice and banana, with no suspicion it's
a breakfast as bad as any cake or doughnut.

So, even as I make my mother's lunch,
or help her get up to find her mostly own
way to the bathroom, I'm also trying
to teach my father, quietly, in a house
that has known only yelling, how to cut
out a few carbs, add a few proteins
to his late winter days, at least until
he can get back to work his garden,
when the last snow has left him one
more winter less to lament.

I make him hard-boiled eggs, easy
to grab one with each breakfast, a ready-made
mid-day snack, even though
my sisters say he won't listen.
A day before I'm set to leave
the eggs are gone, so I boil more final signs
to my father his son showed up
to worry about his old parents
in person, to do the too little he could
for the too little time left to do it.

Five Days Before His 91st Birthday

. . . I dreamed my father was painting
 the interior of our beat-up garage,
and I came up to him and asked
if he thought it was wise to work

so hard just after his release
from the hospital for his second heart attack
in five weeks. He just kept painting,
off-white over tired light

green, but he looked at me
without his anger,
and showed a sort of gentle regard
for me having traveled so far to measure

how much I cared, and then, of course,
I awoke twelve hundred miles
away from where my father lies
in bed back home, a third heart attack

away, perhaps, from never
getting up again, while I sit here
composing and the garage shivering
without its new coat.

After My Brother Claimed I Was Tough

at our father's wake, where we reminisced with
Gerard McCabe and Billy Abruzzino, two of Mike's
old friends I hadn't seen in thirty years, I figured
he was being kind or forgetful, but he insisted,
"You were, man, you were tough when you needed to be,"

and this coming from a cop who has to feel fearless
every moment "on the job" so maybe, I thought,
he meant what he was pitching with his usual self-
assurance, me, a professor of poetry in a family full
of cops, plumbers, construction workers, like our dad

"Two By Four Joe," who once settled a dispute
with an endangering co-worker by a pow
of hard wood across the head. And so
I remembered the time Mike, age eight, charged
into our bedroom, breathless, claiming a bunch

of what passed for my friends were making
our father out a schmuck for giving me the MVP trophy
for CYO softball, hardware they said should have gone
to Ricky Irizarry, that same scrub who hadn't even
played much the year before my father's gruff sympathy

rescued him to our team. I put down my book,
took my skinny self out to insist they stop their bullying,
take back their lies, as I challenged each of them
in turn to fight, heard all four back down, saw
my kid brother's eyes shine, trusting I had something

of our father available those times I might most need it.

After My First Bad Slice of Pizza

Just three weeks into my new life in Columbus:
first apartment, graduate school, newlywed woman
so concerned with getting her field sites set before
the first frost she left me with our apartment's flat roof
leaking through a light fixture over our bed to hop

on her bicycle (we had no car) and head towards
the Olentangy and the jewel-weeds and thistle whose
company she already seemed to prefer to mine. Still, I'd been
told this first year was toughest, had already made friends,
Candis and Mike, veteran English grad students, wanting

my help to move. They had literal tons of stuff besides
the piano, but I never minded other people's moves,
no headache for me, hardly any back ache, even, at 21,
plus Mike promised a beer and pizza party after
we sweated everything over. I've never been fussy

about beer brands, but the first bite I took of the pizza
they had delivered with absolutely no hint of malice
in either their Ohio or Carolina blue eyes, came close
to making me cry, tasting a lot like the last
straw, or cut-out cardboard with too sweet tomato paste,

since in all my twenty-one years before
of Italian mother's homemade or NYC
pizzerias, I had never figured there
could be this kind of sad surprise
awaiting me. So much I had assumed was certain

I could never be certain of again.

TEACHER AND CHILDREN

Song

"She sang a song without any questions, full of color and joy."
                                        –Elisa Kleven

It isn't easy to sing that way,
since song suggests word and all
words can be questions.
And she was not naïve.
She wasn't singing without knowing
why we worry about any joy
asking us to accept it
without inquisition.

And yet her song seemed
satisfied to suggest its colors
proved how natural it also is
to sing. Rainbows are real:
though no more believable
than killing storms, no less
so, either.

Her singing said suspend
your doubts, breathe in belief,
make your very listening a prayer
of thanks someone can still sing
this way, and you will co-create
these colors,
join this joy.

Fohey and Joey

"Vaudeville... n 1.a. Stage entertainment offering a variety
of acts, such as slapstick turns, song, and dance routine, and
juggling performances."
–American Heritage Dictionary

Their slapstick seemed most natural—
both tall, with long arms, prominent
noses, eyes sad enough for any comedy.
Singing and dancing took practice—
few knew how many times she had to suffer
his songs before she could render them back,
in a smaller, truer voice, nor how often
they could not help giggling at each other's
footwork, before they accustomed themselves
to the rhythms in time's embrace.
Juggling, though that's what they managed best-
what a marvel to see them keep aloft
half a dozen objects of various sizes
and shapes, any one of which might have spelled
injury, even doom, if they let
it slip, like a comic kiss missing
lips, smacking the ground
with a well-timed thud.
Oh, they were really
really good—it makes me forever
unwilling to accept
Vaudeville is dead.

Apricots

They looked like undernourished peaches;
their skins' shriveled taste did nothing to convince
me I was wrong, so I have no summery childhood
fondness for this fruit, no stories to tell,
until last year at Half Moon Bay,
last leg of a long scenic car view
of America with my tall, green-eyed girlfriend.
We shared the Pacific, its pounding waves,
azure-endless horizon broken up
by brown pelicans at rest on dark boulders.
We stopped at a diner run by a big family
of Portuguese, warm to regulars
and wanderers alike—one of the best
lunches of my life—first a thick turkey sandwich
with cranberry sauce on homemade bread, then
for dessert, a large slice of fresh-made apricot pie.
Crust flaky, firm, flavorful at once, fruit more poten
than any peach, taste more exotic than any apple
pie could offer, and so all the more American.

Now when I open a jar of apricot
preserves, spread some on a grateful bagel,
the color, taste, takes me away from February.
I smile, look to my green-eyed wife, knowing
it is never too late to discover
the sweetness of summer,
its patient, fruitful bounty.

After I Left the Hospital Having Witnessed the Birth of My First Child

Four in the morning the fourth of June the weather
was cold, early March cold, with pouring
rain. That soaking summer of 1993, weeks later the levee
would break and almost drown West Quincy,
but I was somewhere else,

flooded with the almost thirty-eight years of my life
before this moment: the teen years contemplating
the priesthood, mostly because I could not believe
any woman would ever want me, the eleven years
of the first marriage, where we might as well

have been celibate, my first wife so protective
against pregnancy. And the years swimming away
up to Aunt Flo's funeral in Oklahoma, where I went
and witnessed the soothing dignity
of family, the mourning of my five cousins,

the honor they delivered in allowing me
to escort their feeble father through the ceremonies,
while they pall-bore their loved one to her final place.
In that sea of suits and ties and dark
dresses, I recognized my own children drowning,

but not too late for a life-
saver, the lightning strike divorce no
betrayal, instead an inevitable stirring,
a storm cycle designed before my beginning,
this rainy night bequeathing to me

my daughter's cries, already calling me by my nighest name.

Sudden Rain

My student, who often arrives late,
today also arrives wet, amazing me,
since when I left my office, one of the few
with a big window, it was white
clouds, blue sky, and some sun.
People are reading each other's
poems, so no one minds as I slip out
to find how wet it is getting
since the guy grading our yard
in hopes of halting our periodic
basement pond stopped when
four inches of rain crashed
at once on his big yellow
Caterpillar. He can't come back
until all the mud dries back to earth.
So when I open the door to my office
for the best look at this latest dampening
to my modest hopes, I'm embarrassed
by the rainbow, brightening across campus,
humbling as any undeserved present,
and I see a student I like, sitting, waiting
to talk to someone else, and I invite:
"Want to see a rainbow?" He smiles and notices
there are two, just a little
piece of sky apart, which I had missed
at first, but which, nonetheless, were
there all the time.

The Plant in My Office

is the first I've ever kept
more than a year alive
of the thirty I've breathed
there.

No flowers interrupt
the green, long leaves,
lower ones drooping, the rest
reaching towards the absent
sky.

I'm unaware of what kind
of plant resides with me,
nor whether it could grow
tree-sized if transported
to free soil or at least a bigger
pot.

Only wanting water once
a week, shedding only a few
leaves at a time, after they have
become tan ghosts of their former
selves. This plant's an easy roommate
its sturdy brown base promising years
more.

I sometimes mistake
its single drops of sticky sap
poised on any number of its stems
for tears, though there is no way
of knowing if my planted companion
cries more for its own sake or
mine.

After Seeing My Son Dance a Tarantella in Fairfield, Iowa

whose only Italian-Americans are east and west
coast transplants who moved for the Meditation
Center at Mararishi U. Still, they reverence
their roots enough to take over the small town
square once a year for "All Things Italian,"

including semi-authentic renditions of lasagna
biscotti, cannoli, opera singers from Iowa City,
a zampogna player (that's an Italian bagpipe
if you're wondering), and me, who they import
from small-town Missouri to deliver

my diaspora stories and poems from years
back in Brooklyn and Queens. This time there's
also a folk-dancing troupe from Des Moines,
led by a woman who at almost 80, is still lively,
reminding me a lot of my just dead Aunt Louise.

This paisana, peasant-costumed like the rest,
announces the selections and keeps time
on a tambourine, while young, Midwest Italian-Americans
launch one folk dance after another, with more than one
tarantella, the one my relatives would recall throughout my childhood

at all their celebrations. When it was time
for audience participation, my sixteen-year-old son,
named after his grandfather, got up and literally
gave it a whirl, making me dizzy with thanks
at how gracefully he took to that old dance,

with no self-conscious concern of where any of us were.

After We Noticed the Little Redbud Tree

and its pinkish-purple response to April, catching
whatever sun it could, wedged as it was
between our shed and some adult oaks,
we recognized it as the natural
result of our having spread seeds

from its mother in the middle
of our yard, whose bean-like pods
we've plucked yearly, with each of our
four children, to scratch free the waxy green
seeds (which are pale white if plucked too soon,

mahogany when left alone longer) and place
them anywhere we thought they might sprout
without getting annihilated by a lawn mower. Each child
has cherished this simple effort to spread some new life
into the world, each gotten old enough to want to pluck down

the lower pods herself or himself, free the seeds
and send them somewhere possible. Sometimes
three or four of us have been outside at once,
wondering if there was really a chance,
so now we are thankfully uncertain which one

was responsible for the little tree
we know will soon enough unlock its heart-
shaped leaves, tolerating some shade
to inhabit this unlikely corner
for its living as a certain sign

of ever advancing Spring.

Bobwhite on Our Back Lawn

We don't live
in the woods
anymore, nor
very near a farm-
house, so a quail
in College Park
surprises.

Small, grey-brown
bird, yet bigger
than our ordinary robins,
blue jays, and wrens.
Only twenty seconds
worth of watching before she
skips

through a gap in the fence
to uncover whatever the next
yard offers, not time enough
to point her out to everyone
in our house hiding from
the heat. The air conditioner sounding
sadder somehow than it did
just the moment before.

Solo

I like the waves of sound,
harmonies, communal chords
of a good chorus.

Even more, a guitar
or two, several singers
owning a lyric together
is something happy to hear.

Yet for me singing most seems
a solitary thing, remembering how
I kept my life intact my teenage years
composing confessions to Sylvia
or later Hallene, not expecting
they would ever hear them.

And now hardly a night passes
when I don't listen to sixteen-year-old
Claire's solitary singing in her room,
accompanied by the guitar I bought her,
taught her to play, her voice secure
in the insecurity of its longing,
her truest sounds speaking to the world,
but mostly hers alone.

Pasta Three Times a Week

Except back in Queens we called it macaroni,
no matter the shape: rotini, farfalle, even
Ma's homemade cavatelli, and the sauce we called
gravy, also homemade, my grandmother's recipe.

Every Sunday, my mother would start that sauce
in the morning before Mass, and we'd eat our main
meal in the early afternoon.
There would be meatballs, sausage, maybe a piece
of pork swimming in that sauce, but with seven
children, a husband, frequent Sunday guests,
hardly any meat would survive with the leftover
sauce we'd have for Wednesday's supper.

So my mother fashioned "eggballs," invented
during the Depression by her mother,
meatless meatballs, football-shaped concoctions
of romano, breadcrumbs, eggs, a little parsley,
soaked through with the red sauce, too much softer
than poverty to make meatlessness a shame.

Friday too we usually had pasta,
instead of fish, but without meat
sauce, even after the Pope said
it was okay; after all, the price
of ground chuck didn't go down
with the dispensation.

My wife, four children, and I
we're down to just two times,
still Sunday and Wednesday, though,
still eggballs to offset the missing meat,

hoping to teach them something
by reliving the simple bounty
of my past, our present
lives together.

$40 Cake

The cake was as beautiful as the fancy
place I bought it from.

Maybe I should have bought one
soaked with Kirsch or rum.

This one was not moist or dense
or flavorful.

This cake was corporate, and dry,
its frosting heavy without nuance.

My children who live near the fancy
bakery so wanted it to be better.

My children felt embarrassed for all
the money I had spent on a mediocre cake.

It wasn't their fault; I had insisted;
I had longed for an exceptional, big-city dessert.

The cheese Danish my daughter had bought
for our lunch at home was better.

The cakes any one of us knows how to
scratch at home are always better.

The cake cost $42+ if you count
the tax.

My disappointment, my chagrin:
one cannot affix a price.

We still ate the cake;
it took two different meals to end it.

The memory lingers, a bitter after-
taste, like unsweetened chocolate.

I Wear an Eight Dollar Watch

Since I own no cell
phone I need something
to keep up to date.

My desk drawer sequesters
four watches that cost much
more but whose time has run out.

The watch I wear says simple:
black face, white numbers,
with a tiny "water resistant" pledge.

I don't like to swim and won't wear
the watch while washing dishes, but still,
it's quite a claim for under ten dollars.

Of course, my computer also knows
what time it is, even does daylight savings
by itself but stops reporting while full-screened.

I like how little the watch cost me;
I like how it's still running well after a year;
I like how I don't have to worry about replacing the battery.

When it wants to rest with the rest
of the old watches in the drawer, I'll just place
it there and get its younger brother,

probably "new and improved"
still a certain bargain for less than ten
for all that telling on time.

Mrs. Barber's Memory

This nice old lady we visit
at Kirksville Manor Care,
seems like one of the ones better
off. Though in a wheelchair, she
isn't ruled by chronic pain, roams
the halls, visits rooms occupied
by those few others able to hold
coherent conversations.
She doesn't even have dietary restrictions,
can eat any cake, cookies, candy
we remember to bring.

We only get there once a week,
Friday afternoons, not enough
for her to recall us at once,
but when we get talking
she is happy, especially with the children,
who don't mind answering the same questions
each week.

Although she can recall small
details from her childhood
in Cedar Rapids, and the words
to every song she's ever learned,
she thinks Christmas is past when
it hasn't, can no longer judge distance
from sorrow. Last week, we found her
sad, alone, in her little room,
blue over having lost her husband
the week before, when it has really
been three years—her brain betraying
her to experience again
and again the key losses
of her life.

Metaphysicians have ever dwelt
on the foggy unreality of time.
Now so too, Mrs. Barber.

After Having That Italian Pastry Dream for About the Hundredth Time

The one where I'm walking down Liberty Avenue
in search of an open bakery and I either get lost
because the should-be-straightforward avenue
takes unnatural turns away from the familiar
and I wander, afraid, confused, liable to be mugged

or I find bakeries closed
or featuring nothing
a normal New York Italian bakery offers:
cannoli, chocolate eclairs, napoleons,
sfogliatelle, sfingi di San Giuseppe,

rum cakes, biscotti, sesame seed
or pignoli cookies.
Nothing of what I long for
here in small-town Missouri
over a thousand miles away

from my favorite foods, though
who wouldn't conclude this frequent fantasizing
over what I can only get on too rare
returns to Queens
means something more serious

than gluttony or missing my past,
since the bakeries never supply me
with what I seek, since I always end up
unsatisfied, since a few times
I've even been badly beaten

for never learning to just stop trying.

After Keith and I Stopped Meeting in
front of Macy's on Christmas Eve

breaking a streak of eighteen straight years
of late morning meetings, with all the nations of New York
City seeming to stream out of the corner subway station
until one of them would be Keith. I was sad to see
it end, but believed we'd pick it up again just as soon

as the first two kids got a little older. Instead,
my wife decided traveling all that way by van, Kirksville
to NYC, was too tricky on winter I-80. So we stayed
each December, to be with my in-laws in even smaller
Palmyra, where there is no need for a subway, and everybody

looks the same. The hours Keith and I would roam
the center of my old hometown seemed stolen as we sampled
Sicilian pizza, knishes, cannoli, and other nourishment Kirksville
can't offer. We considered anything cash or credit card
could buy for last-minute gifts. Sometimes we'd visit

St. Patrick's, MOMA, and the Hudson, as we long-walked
each other through the year gone by, as I reconnected
to the pure pace and movement of Manhattan at the holidays.
I'd always have to stop too soon, book back to the A
rumbling me to my parents' place in time for the fish

dinner rites of Christmas Eve night in an Italian-American home.
How should I have known, when I agreed to give it up for easier,
safer plans that I could never claim again the throb connecting
me to all those strangers flowing up from below the ground,
seeking like me the one I could recognize as a particular friend,

lost to me now forever in some space I can't call home.

After Margaret Did Not Believe How Soon Forsythias Turn Green

"Margaret are you grieving,
Over Goldengrove unleaving?"
                    –Gerard Manley Hopkins, "Spring and Fall"

Margaret was not grieving over golden
flowers deceiving as they gloried
bushes before leaving them emerald
into Fall. At six, she could not
remember how soon April

makes December, how redbud,
magnolia, and dogwood splendor
hardly lasts more than a week.
Margaret loves the forsythias'
little yellow flowers adorning

ours and neighbors' bushes,
collecting them, selecting also
tiny violets, and other woodland wild
flowers to adorn an orange
juice glass proud to become a vase.

Blue-purple, white-pink, and gold, these tiny
blossoms stay bright as long as their outdoor
cousins but soon top trash ready for discarding,
as Margaret's miscalculations of how long
Spring blossoms linger, will work themselves

away, naturally as May kneels towards
summer's passion. This year, though, she will
probably lament how soon the maples, oaks,
and hickories lose their leaves' final fire. For me,
resignation leaves nothing left to long for,

so it is Margaret I mourn for.

THE CRACKER BOX

After We Finally Called the Bat Men

whose Batmobile was a sky blue pick-up truck
with black bats painted all around, and whose expertise
had us bat-free in a week, I wished we had found them
sooner, so the first fifteen years in our house in the woods
would not have been so rich in flying rodents.

Two of my sisters were visiting for the first time;
I figured Annmarie had to be nightmaring when
she woke us at three to report a bat in the guest room,
but then it dive-bombed my head in the narrow hallway
and soon we were all ducking or screaming or both.

The Little Brown Bat looks a lot bigger when it's flying
in your house; we averaged one or two a year, usually
in summer, but no day or night was immune to the possibility.
Once at halftime of a Jets-Broncos playoff game, we heard
wind chimes we'd hung in the downstairs family room

warning us we had another visitor. We'd hear them scratching in the attic
scurrying in the walls, never knowing when one might make its way out or why.
We closed off the fireplace, sealed gaps in the garage without avail.
One swooped in right in the middle of "Lassie Come Home." I got mad,
gave up trying to catch and release, took to taking them out of the air with
a broom. I grew skilled; my bashing

a fallen bat with that broom was a welcome signal to my wife
and children that it would soon be safe to come back out. A reluctant hero,
I once closed myself in the bathroom with the intruder we saw fly in;
I had to dispatch that one with a towel in the bathtub where the lights
had stunned it. I never guessed I could transform into a mass murderer,
an anti-ecologist:

scary what a home, wife and children, will insist you become.

After Taking the Wrong I-480 Out of Omaha

instead of a quick hook up to I-29 towards Kansas City
we ended up off the highway onto some local road
wounded with construction for many miles. Rand McNally
promised we would find a toll bridge back to 29 if
we kept straight towards Plattsmouth, but

when we got there, no signs showed the way to recover
the interstate. I first found direction from the tired woman
behind the Quik-Trip counter: lefts and rights leading
to the old, unmarked truck route, she promised, would
take us to the Toll, but somehow, we missed a turn

and ended up at the town square, mostly closed for Sunday,
where a young couple pointed out how we'd gone wrong.
The Toll Bridge, $1.25 one way, was as rusty as the old man
who took our money as if awakened from our dream, surely the first
business he'd had for hours. Even the mighty Missouri looked

nondescript in Plattsmouth, Nebraska, its brown waters gently waving
at us from below. Still, there was no sign for I-29 after
we were off the old structure. But we feigned faith and found
what we sought some miles later. Later still, some research
uncovered that prairie town was the boyhood home of

Raymond Chandler, author of *The Big Sleep*, and other
marvelous mysteries, someone I thought had gotten
all his darkness from London and Los Angeles, someone
who, ages 2-7, also might have sought an escape, though
Plattsmouth featured no signs admitting that either, while

we looked for that only bridge out of town.

The Pit Bulls of East Oakland

eat better than the homeless who wander International Ave.,
five of whom hit me up for spare change while I walked
with my Catholic Worker daughter in search of the transient burrito
truck on a cool, tense evening in August.

They are, after all, large, sleek and murderous
status symbols of the residential neighborhood off International,
where blacks and Latinos both elect them to almost mythic
power in the protection of their modest homes and showy cars.

My daughter has to walk their gauntlet each morning on her way
to work for the poor, passing pooches famous for the power
of their death-friendly jaws, Maria only one careless move away
from the open gate to a horrible ending.

I grew up in Jamaica, Queens, a place at least as unsteady
as this one where we kept dogs too for protection against robbers
and worse, but some of ours were small, since we understood
most any bark or bite suffices to warn the bad away.

Instead, these owners court the worst results
taking pride in the casual lethalness
of canines who, after a day or two of our tourist
walking, didn't even bother to get up

to protest our approach, knowing as only
dogs might, how unlikely we were to be
threats to their domains. Still, the ones
owned by Spanish speakers seem to reserve

the right to snarl at any black person passing,
even as one of those black men jokes when
he sees our family walking by his place, "Damn,
my rent is going to go up now for sure,"

knowing as he does how East Oakland
sits just a few developers away from
sharing the fate of most of Brooklyn,
a whitewash of Yuppies, a rejection of soul

food, pupusas, churros rellenos in favor
of things white folks prefer, including
a richer variety of dogs, other safeguards
to keep the undesired at bay.

The Silence of the Wrens

only happens after the sun submits
to the usual darkness. All day they
are louder than tiny birds seem capable,
and with a brood this June morning
in the little house we always leave for them,
they are much noisier still.

For many years we have enjoyed the sights
and sounds of their frenetic chattering
flights to and from home base, all the while
worrying when larger birds pose threats.

For the past two years, a pair of English sparrows,
who we've read will kill wrens when they can,
have malingered near, even upon the wren house.

How easy it is for people to make pat fiction
from nature: the evil, non-native ruffians I've
tried to scare away without bothering "our" birds,
even my sense the wrens appreciate the support.

If only I hadn't read while looking up how long
wrens live: these birds are infamous themselves
for cracking the eggs of other parents in their neighborhood,
even those of other wrens.

Lacking the motives of even a crow or jay,
who break eggs to eat them, these wrens
just murder to keep down the competition,
as if our yard lacked little bugs in mid-summer.

And so, I prefer their silence allowing
me to forego my foolishness, though my resentment
extends it since these little liars only do what their DNA
demands, an excuse all killers have but one, so I must leave
their little house alone.

I Hit a Squirrel with a Child's Green Plastic Watering Can

from my deck to the feeder below, fifteen feet away,
knocking him off his precarious perch and onto the green
grass blackened by the remains of myriad sunflower seeds.

If I were hit by an unnatural green missile, I think I'd run,
maybe to the wide red cedar where he and all his rodent
and avian fellow feeders usually seek cover.

He stands his ground, though, not dazed nor hurt,
with a calm, dark gaze that seems to say, "Is that all you
got, old man?"

I've been chasing squirrels off a dozen times a day
with everyone else in the household wondering
why I would bother.

They keep the birds I want to see away: the rose-
breasted grosbeaks, the goldfinch, and the cardinals
all keep their colors to themselves, in fear of fox and gray squirrels.

If I were a hunter, I guess they would be easy prey,
but I'm not, and they know it, so they keep coming back
no matter how far off the deck I run or what I might heave from it.

My only consolation is the accuracy of that one toss, though even
that feels more like a carnival trick, the one where you knock down
all the pins but receive some crummy prize

from the squirrely guy in charge
laughing to himself about having
fleeced yet one more fool.

After Claire Asked Me to Teach
Her How to Play Guitar

I recalled that I too was twelve when I first learned from my older
cousin Sammy Todaro, who taught guitar in his parents' finished
basement, surrounded by his father's banjos and mandolins; he halved
his normal two dollars a lesson charge since I was family. I learned
from for two years enough to get competent with chords
to accompany myself

to almost any song I wanted badly enough
to sing, including those I wrote myself, imagining
someday others might hear and sing them.
Claire loves The Beatles, and has worked hard to take
What I could teach and turn it into "Eleanor Rigby,"

"In My Life," "The Fool on the Hill," "I Will." In less
than two years, she's gotten really good and is getting better
all the time. She has her own guitar now and a big Beatles book
in her basement bedroom, though she can also play everything
from "The Lily of the West" to "Crazy" songs

she's learned from her older brother's prompting, a singer
without the patience to work to play. When I think Claire
making music, I look back to patient Cousin Sammy, now two months
dead, who played guitar in wedding bands and gave lessons
but could never earn a living just doing what he loved. Now I see
those hour-long

lessons were not for money. He was passing
on melody and rhythm and hope, showing
me how I could use my hands, my muscle memory,
my callused fingers to get a crafted wooded box
to sing. He was entrusting to me, as his father to him,

the confident chords I now hear rising up from my daughter's room.

A-Fib and the Fly

"I heard a Fly buzz-when I died"
                              –Emily Dickinson

Two-fifty AM and my first arrhythmia in nine months.

I've had this condition since before I was fifty, but back then
the doctors said after my cardiac catheterization showed
how wide my arteries were, I had little to worry about,
particularly since I always settled back to sinus rhythm.

Now, though, experts inside my treacherous television exclaim
even five minutes of atrial fibrillation greatly increases
the chance of a stroke, so instead of sleeping through
this bout, I stay awake waiting for the numbness,
the tingling towards the potential panicked call
to the ER.

I go to the bathroom further from where my wife sleeps
so as not to awaken or worry her.
As I sit contemplating my mortality from the toilet seat,
I consider all the ironies: a friend not ten hours earlier
telling me about an acquaintance younger than us who died
in her sleep during a trip to Acapulco;
the line I used when the cleaning woman at work remarked
on all the people my age who had retired recently: "Yeah,
they're dropping like flies, but I'm going to try flying a little longer."

This line buzzes most in my brain because of my company:
a fly no happier than I to be awake and feeling trapped inside.
My instinct is to get up to try to swat him, but I get the idea
someone this close to death or debilitation should consider
letting all other life live.

Still, the fly keeps buzzing me, so I do get up, pull my pajama pants
back to go mode, grab a hand towel, and, surprising to us both,
soon have him crushed and in the wastebasket, a black dot in a field
of used white tissues.

In the end, no matter the final outcome awaiting me,
I have chosen to be ruthless,
like life is.

After Singing "Volare" with an Actual Italian

"Penso che un sogno cosí non ritorni mai piú."
                    –Domenico Modugno, "Volare"

Doralisa de Agostini, my American Romanticism student
all the way from Milano, who knew more about Hawthorne
than any of the actual Americans, she helped to pronounce names
like Baglioni (not Bag lee own-e) or especially Beatrice,
all four syllables more beautiful by far when said the right way.

Sujash Purna, from Bangladesh, but, unlike Dora, with plans
to stay in the States, invited me to meet his visiting parents,
share a meal the night before graduation, without informing
me Dora too would be there, her pasta, his stir-fry, my black
raspberry brownie cake, a mixed-up menu together.

I found out that in Bangladesh cake is a treat reserved
for birthdays and was flattered Doralisa had two big slices
of mine, saying it was so much nicer than the dorm food
she had been suffering. I found out Sujash, a first-rate
poet, also sang and played guitar, and wanted to find some common

musical ground. Instead, we had to take turns, the parents even
entertaining us with a sad Bangla song that felt all the more full
of meaning for not knowing what it meant. Doralisa wished too
to sing but didn't know my Italian offerings, "O Sole Mio"
"Oi Mari," foreign to her youth, but thanks to Andrea Bocelli's

reclamation she knew "Volare." Just the two of us sang it together,
"Volare" to fly, "cantare" to sing, her soft alto, my certain bass, producing
somehow "una musica dolce sonando soltanto per noi," two people united
for the first and last time, by two minutes of a song I've known
for most of my life, but only really knew then, that dream

returning "mai piú," which I understand means nevermore.

After Black Friday Began on a Thursday

I wondered if my sisters-in-law,
who have always cracked dawn
on the long drive to the mall in Springfield
the morning after giving thanks would consider
skipping the second turkey at their in-laws

to make the pilgrimage to those merchants
making the holiday's sunset
the beginning of Black Friday's Sabbath,
so they could witness all
the best deals for Christmas

presents, so they could justify
all the workers having to leave
their families early to serve
something besides a second piece of pumpkin
pie to someone even more a stranger

to them than their Uncle Melvin
who remembers when no store owner
could consider opening on Thanksgiving,
or Sunday, for that matter, though this
from a man who doesn't even own a credit card, so why worry

what he remembers? After all, blowing off your in-laws
to shop sales hardly compares to ritual overeating
in a world where many go hungry, to celebrate
white people taking advantage of the hospitality
of a race they would mostly annihilate to make room

for their descendants' appetites and shopping centers.

Ode To January

"To behold the junipers shagged with ice,
The spruces rough in the distant glitter

Of the January sun; and not to think
Of any misery in the sound of the wind..."
                    –Wallace Stevens, "The Snow Man"

Month that murders the Christmas season,
evidenced by blue spruce strewn
near the curb like so many carcasses,
colorful lights no longer illuminating night,
you start our year off ominously,
promising nothing but cold.

People weigh more than they want to even more
beneath your short sun.
College students limp sadly back
to months without their mothers, factory and office
workers awake without hope beyond some
brief vacation, an impossible summer away.

For who can feel future warmth walking
in your snow, slipping on your sidewalk
sleet and ice? The oaks, maples,
sycamores never green,
crocus, purple hyacinth shivering
even at the thought
of breaking through
the hard, brown ground.

A month without reprieve,
no wonder we lose December,
clouding our brains with booze
enough to pretend
the New Year
could ever be Happy.

If I Could Tell This Story

"Till human voices wake us and we drown."
                    –T.S. Eliot, "The Love Song of J. Alfred Prufrock"

of a time long past,
age fifteen, say, when
possibility still sang
too innocently to seem
a siren, I would become

for the measures it would take
to tempt into words
the adolescent more than
fifty years before,
that pimply kid who wrote

sad songs and unrequited love
sonnets in his locked bedroom,
announcing his belief, even through
the most helpless of lyrics,
he had discovered something

worth sharing with the world.
If I end this story, I will startle
like someone wrenched from dreaming,
wondering why in spite of all the intervening
I am still singing the same songs

now knowing exactly
where they are leading.

James's Dream

In it I was married to Isabella Rossellini.

We had a bonny little boy and a small dog.

The dog we bedecked in a Star Wars outfit.

We all lived in Pittsburgh.
James had a factory job.
Isabella and I opened our home to all,
a certain center for good
fellowship, food, and culture
even.

I had a favored, dark green wing-back chair.

I told James I'd never had a nicer dream myself.
I shared with him the time I was a finalist
for a teaching position at the New School, just
when Isabella was taking a few classes there,
how I didn't get the job or ever meet her.

I told James how touched I was by his
surreal regard for me,
so high it could posit my happy marriage
to a woman so beautifully and carelessly refined.

I told James, though, I'd never dress my dog
in any sort of outfit, most especially
not a Star Wars get-up,
unless, of course,
Isabella insisted.

My Son Caught a Twelve Pound Grass Carp

"On purpose?" his Uncle Ross, a Fisheries & Wildlife worker wondered.
Joey nodded how he'd baited his hook with a leaf from a cottonwood tree,
kept casting to where he had seen that big dream rising from the river.

My son finds fishing more fulfilling than breathing and about as necessary.
He will pursue ponds where only bass and bluegill belong, but prefers
the river or vacation ocean forays for their wider range of possibilities.

To someone like my son each cast is a prayer
each retrieve the answer than can feel as empty
as a no, but which the faithful translate always as just not right now.

Then comes the hit, the tug, the resisting weight electrifying
the line with the iridescent glory of life itself soon
scintillating like burning bush fire in your grateful hands.

I Want Out of the Cracker Box Too

I saw a student presentation about Rumi
as a BIPOC poet, and all this time
I had thought Persians were white.

A few months later I'm reading about
Robert Saleh, a Lebanese American, presented
as one of only a few BIPOC NFL head coaches

and wondering whether anyone
has told Marlo Thomas she's been
biracial all these years.

Back in her dad's day, even his pal
Desi Arnaz, though dark and Cuban,
was considered blanco in the States,

since not too many *I Love Lucy*
fans would have very much loved
them as a biracial couple.

So I looked it up: both Persians
and Arabs have been seeking status
as America's newest not-Caucasians,

I even read an article by an Arab-American
about having had enough of being nominally
white without any of the privilege.

At this rate, the Aryans might get
their centuries-old wish to be the only
ones left in the cracker box.

And I don't see why this dark-as-Desi grandchild
of Calabrese peasant immigrants
with almost certainly some Arab, if not Moorish

blood should be forced to configure himself
swimming in the same gene pool as Prince Andrew,
Barry Mills, or even Edith Wharton;

I don't know why I should continue to suffer
the Mafia jokes and chronic mispronouncing
of my name without being able to get

anybody in trouble for it. Still more
I have to wonder why any of us whole
wheat crackers would want to stay stowed away

in that slowly sinking ship. What Greek, Jew, Slav,
Romanian, Magyar, Portuguese, Sicilian, Basque, Celt,
Cypriot, Armenian, Bulgarian, Moldovan,

Andalusian, Albanian, all the many others
never welcomed in first class, should choose
now to drown with the rats?

Author's Biography

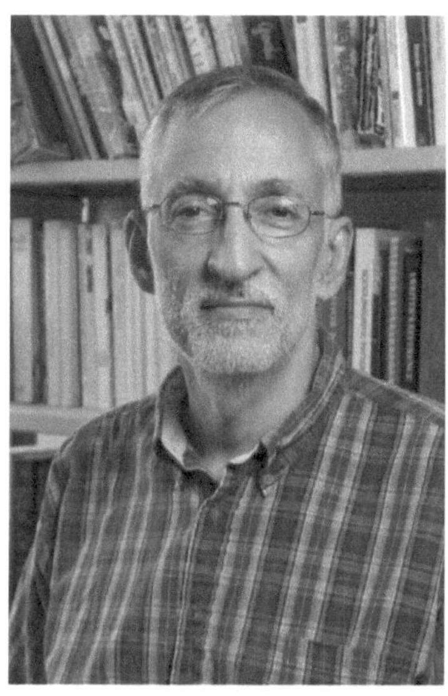

Joe Benevento grew up in a large, Italian-American family in a racially diverse, working-class neighborhood in Queens; a fictionalized version of his times as the only white boy in a large peer group of blacks and Puerto Ricans appears in his 2004 YA novel, *The Odd Squad,* which was a finalist for the John Gardner Fiction Book Award. Benevento went on to major in Spanish and English at NYU, where he graduated magna cum laude, Phi Beta Kappa, before attaining an MA degree in English at Ohio State and a Ph.D. in English at Michigan State. Since 1983 he has taught American literature (including Latinx and Latin American literature in translation), creative writing and Mystery at Truman State University. He is also the long-time poetry editor of the *Green Hills Literary Lantern.* Benevento's poems, stories, essays and reviews have appeared in over 300 journals and magazines, including *Bilingual Review, Slipstream, Cold Mountain Review, Switchback, South Dakota Review, Prairie Schooner, Italian Americana* and *Poets & Writers.* He has fourteen books to his credit, including *Expecting Songbirds: Selected Poems, 1983-2015.* Benevento and his wife Carol live in Kirksville, Missouri, where they have raised four children, Maria, Joseph, Claire and Margaret.